Scott Joplin
Favorites for
Classical Guitar

Arranged and compiled by **Jerry Willard**.

Contents

HAL•LEONARD®

Introduction

The celebrated Ragtime pianist Scott Joplin was born in Texas *c.*1867. Joplin's father Giles, a slave, was given his freedom in his late teens, and at age 18 he met Florence Givens, a freeborn African American. They were married by 'jumping over the broom', the only type of marriage ceremony available to black people at that time. Both musical, Giles played the violin and Florence sang and played the banjo. All five of their children were also musical but it soon became apparent that Scott, their second child, was especially gifted. He was able to pick out tunes on the banjo when he was five, and by the age of seven he could play the instrument fluently. He had perfect pitch and an incredible, near-photographic memory.

It is believed that the young Scott Joplin had access to a piano in the home where his mother worked, and taught himself the basics of music. A local music teacher, Julius Weiss, noticed Joplin's talent and furthered his studies, emphasizing European musical forms including opera.

At a young age, Joplin began working with minstrel troupes playing piano, guitar, and cornet. In 1894 he settled in Sedalia, Missouri, where he played for various social clubs. One was appropriately called the Maple Leaf, soon to be the title of his most famous rag, and the other was the Black 400 Club. In Sedalia he taught piano and guitar. He also taught several well-known ragtime composers, notably Scott Hayden and Arthur Marshall. It is said that Joplin's appearance at the Chicago World's Fair in 1893 helped to establish ragtime as a musical art form. In 1895 he formed a vocal group called the Texas Medley Quartette and toured east to Syracuse, New York. There he published his first songs, 'Please Say You Will' and 'A Picture of Her Face'.

Joplin continued to publish his music and in 1899 he published his most famous piece, 'Maple Leaf Rag', bringing him great fame and a profound influence on other ragtime composers and American music. 'Maple Leaf Rag' brought Joplin a steady but modest income for life. The rag 'The Strenuous Life' (included in this volume) was dedicated to Theodore Roosevelt to commemorate the invitation of Booker T. Washington to the White House, the first time an African American had been invited there. Joplin also composed an opera, *A Guest Of Honor*, to commemorate that event. The score to this opera is believed to be lost and was likely confiscated to pay for Joplin's debts. Throughout his life Joplin suffered from financial difficulties, largely because he never changed his style of playing or writing to suit current trends and fashions. Ragtime had become assimilated into the culture and the style of playing ragtime had changed. Joplin was so concerned about what he considered to be negative influences in ragtime that he published a method, *The School Of Ragtime,* to instruct people on how to play ragtime properly. In 1910 he began to work on another ragtime opera, *Treemonisha.* In 1911, after a favorable review by a well-known opera critic, he began looking for a theater in New York City that would stage it. It was picked up by the Lafayette Theater in Manhattan but, because of management changes, was never produced.

Although during this period he completed some very nice rags, his career was fading. Joplin began exhibiting signs of dementia paralytica, the last stages of syphilis. In January 1917 he was admitted to Manhattan State Hospital where he died on April 1 at the age of 49. He was buried at Saint Michael's Cemetery in East Elmhurst, Queens, New York City, in a grave that remained unmarked until 1974.

Joplin's works include an abundance of rags, waltzes, two operas (*A Guest Of Honor* and *Treemonisha*) a piano concerto, a symphony, a musical comedy, a vaudeville show, and a number of popular songs; sadly most of these are lost. In 1976, Joplin was bestowed posthumously from the Pulitzer Prize Committee a Special Award Citation for his contributions to American music.

The Music

Joplin always wanted to be accepted as a classical composer. Perhaps it was Julius Weiss's influence. Joplin was adamant about his music being played as written and played "not fast" to avoid a novelty feel to the music that was becoming prevalent at that time. Joplin always strived for sophistication and elegance in his music. The primary issue among players today is whether to "swing" the music or not. For example:

The music is written thus:

To swing, it would be played with a lilt written thus:

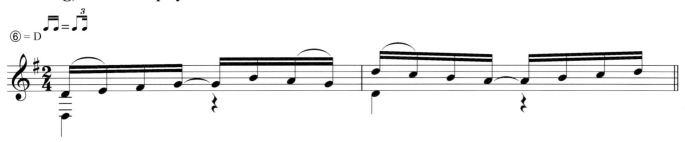

We have piano rolls of Scott Joplin playing his own rags. There is a mixture of both styles but the strict rhythm tends to predominate. I chose to record the rags for this book in a way that would be most effective on the guitar. The guitar has its own ragtime tradition and most of the rags composed for guitar are swung. The guitar easily lends itself to this interpretation, so most of the rags that I have recorded in this book swing, with a few exceptions. In some of the rags I have purposefully done a mixture of both styles to emphasize a phrase or motif that I felt was important. I would recommend the use of a capo with these arrangements for ease of playing, key variety, and sound quality.

The Arrangements

Arranging idiomatic piano music for guitar presents many challenges. One has to determine from the outset how closely one should adhere to the text of the music. I am a firm believer that for a transcription to be successful it must sound as if it's written for that instrument. Two issues in Joplin's piano music presented challenges:

Key Relationships
In the Joplin's ragtime compositional style, he often modulates from the tonic key to the subdominant and/or the dominant key. As a result, I carefully picked keys that would keep open strings available to the guitar. D major, G major, and A major are keys that work well because of the guitar's open strings.

Bass Lines
Because of the smallness of the guitar's range and voice, it is important to define the chord to the ear by using the root immediately. When Joplin chooses to use chord inversions during chord changes, I have decided to use root-position chords to define the chord more clearly, while at the same time trying to maintain the integrity of any moving bass line.

I hope you enjoy learning and playing these lovely rags as much as I did arranging and recording them.

Jerry Willard
New York City, 2014

Cleopha

Music by Scott Joplin

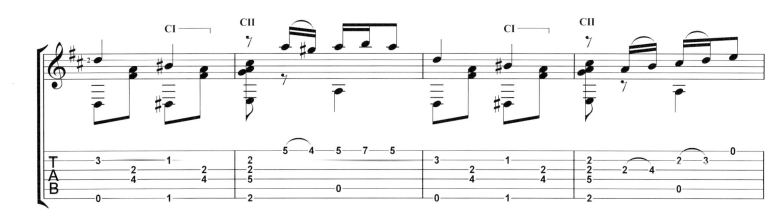

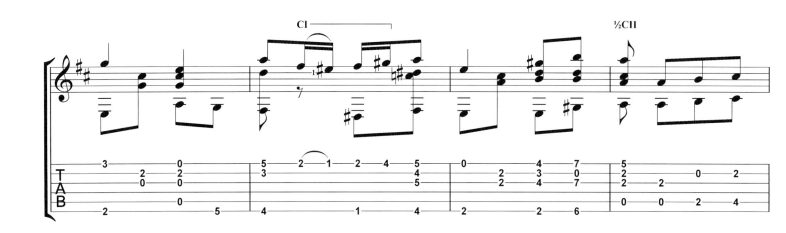

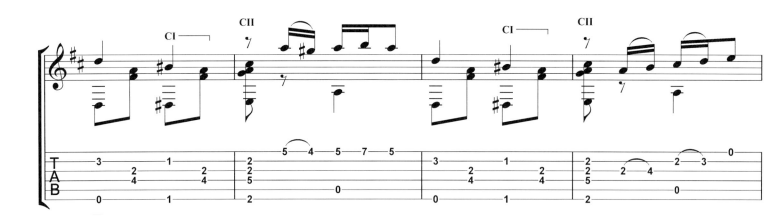

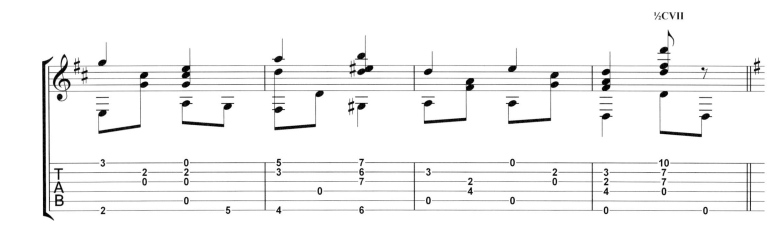

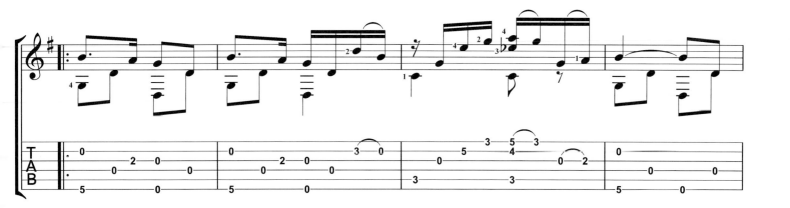

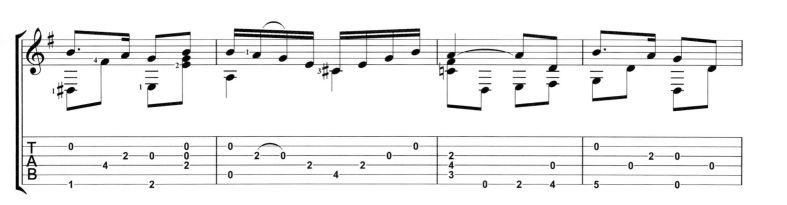

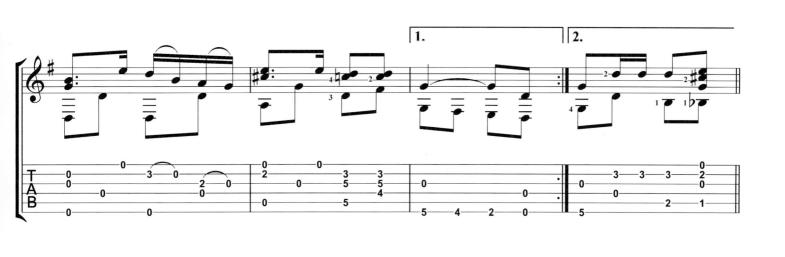

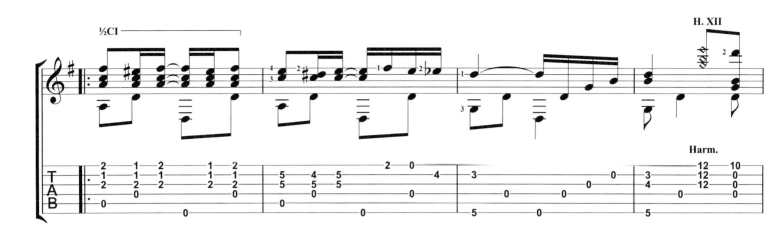

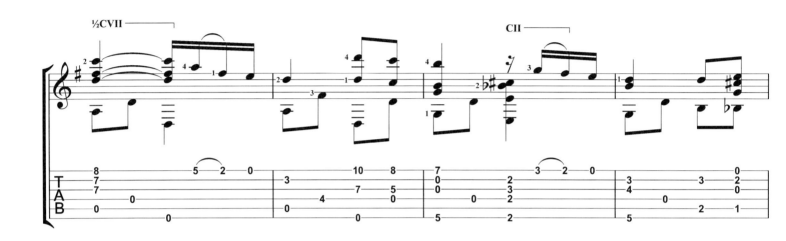

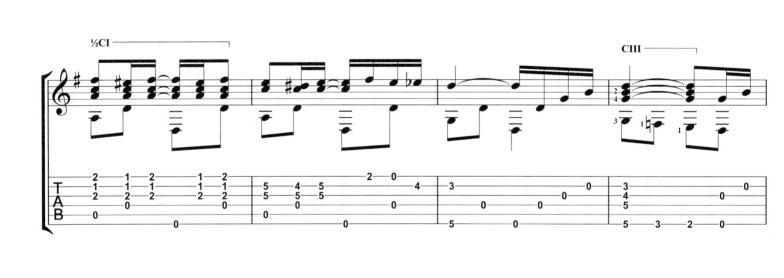

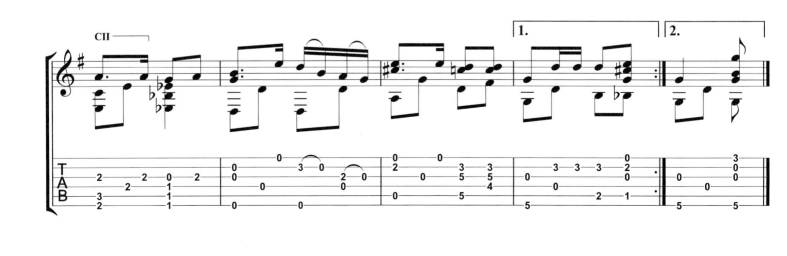

Heliotrope Bouquet

Music by Scott Joplin

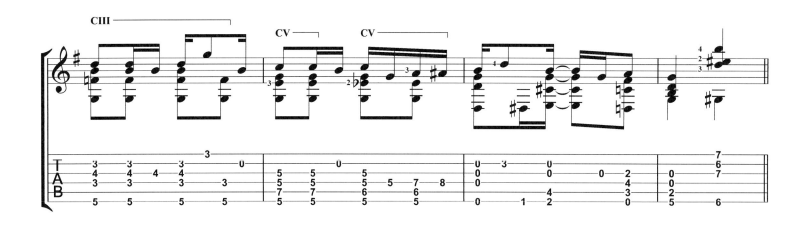

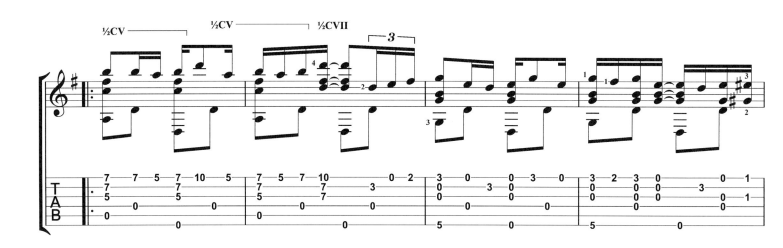

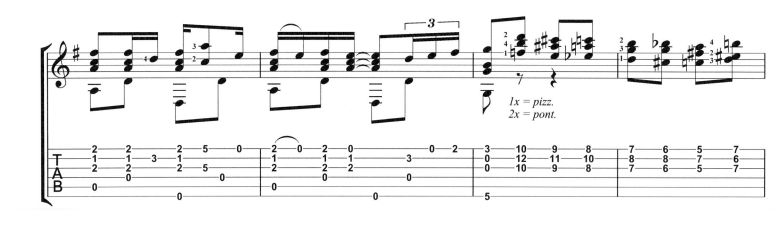

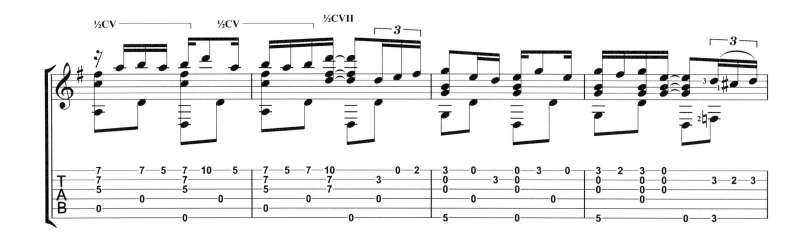

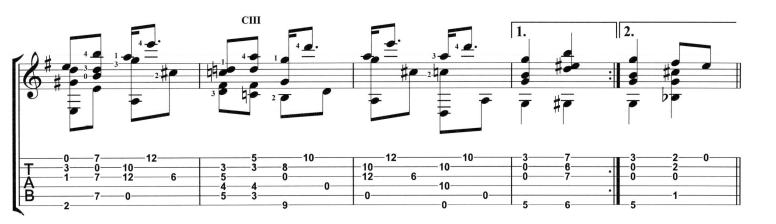

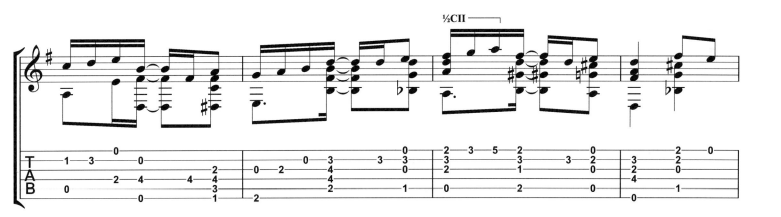

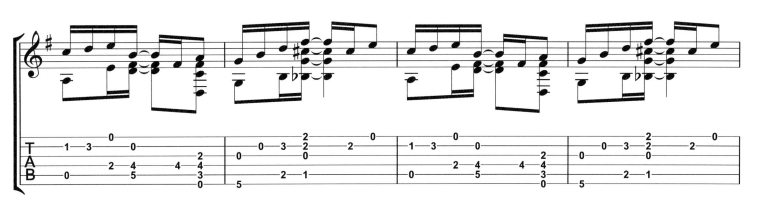

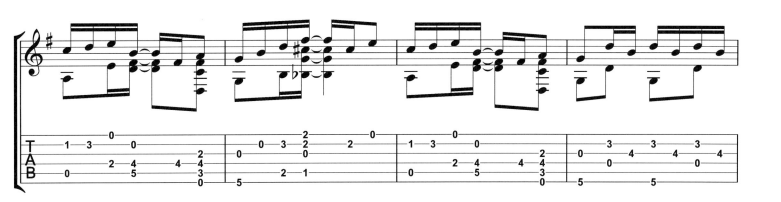

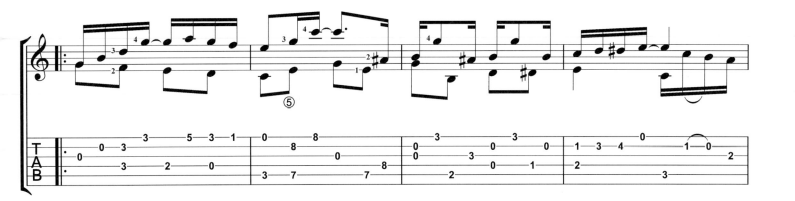

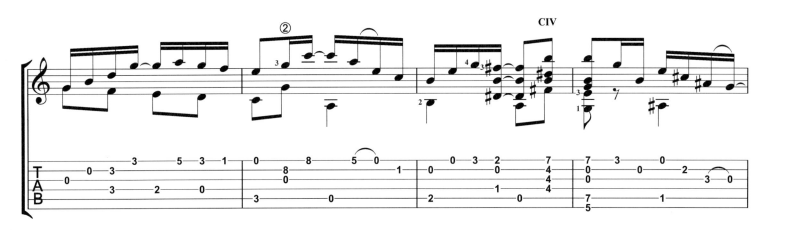

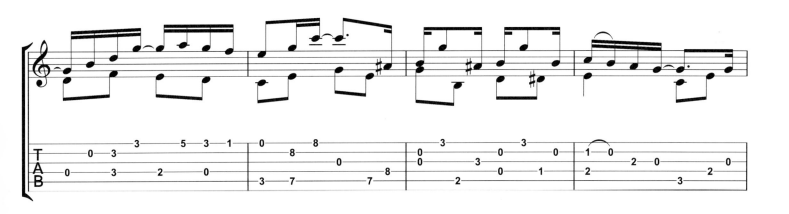

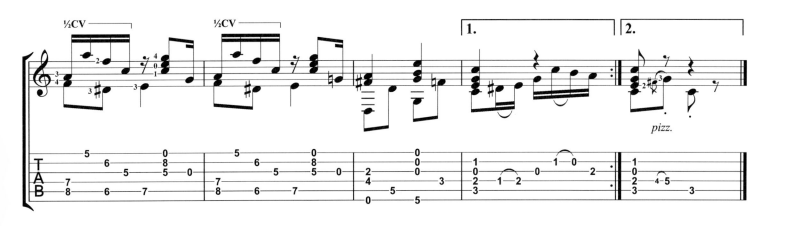

The Entertainer

Music by Scott Joplin

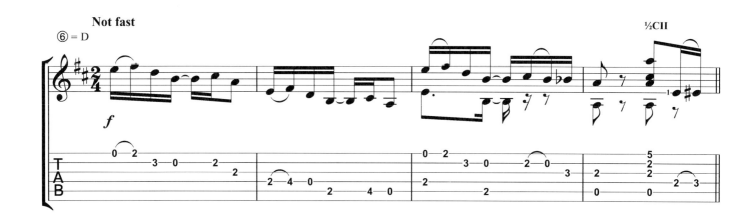

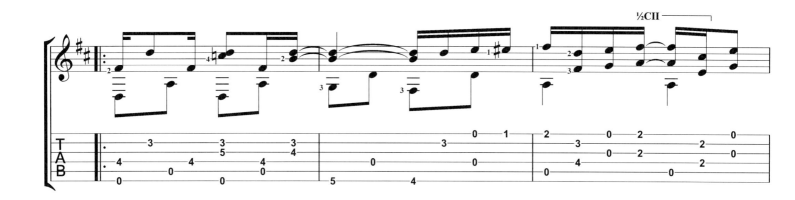

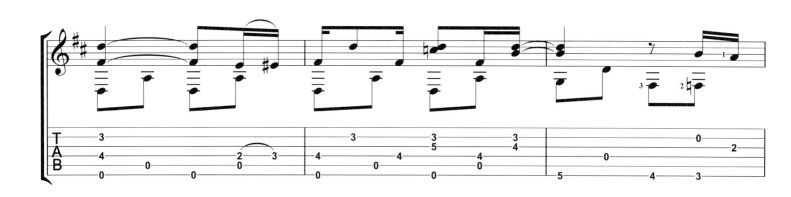

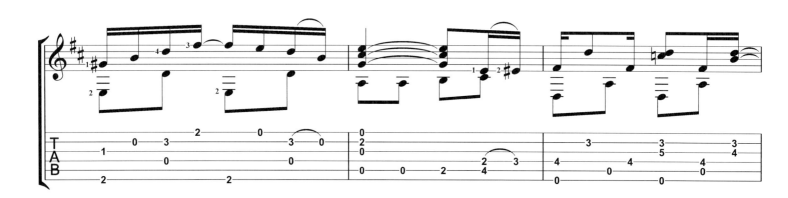

Kismet Rag

Music by Scott Joplin & Scott Hayden

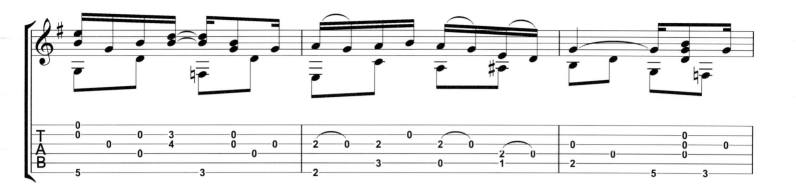

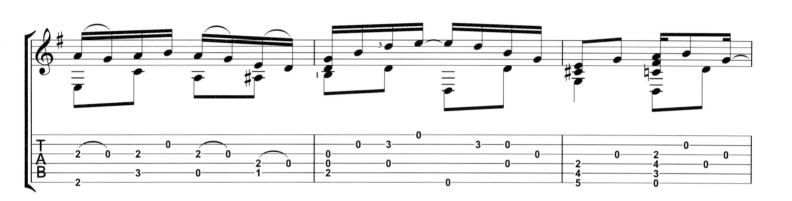

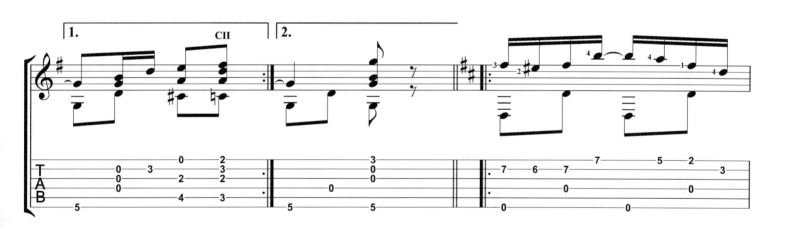

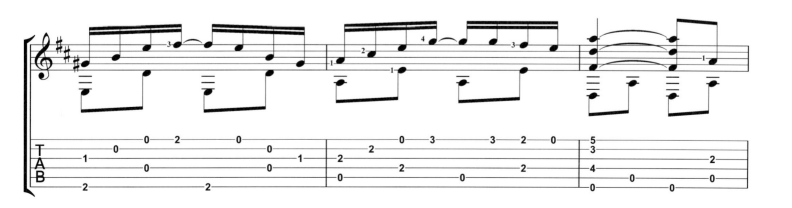

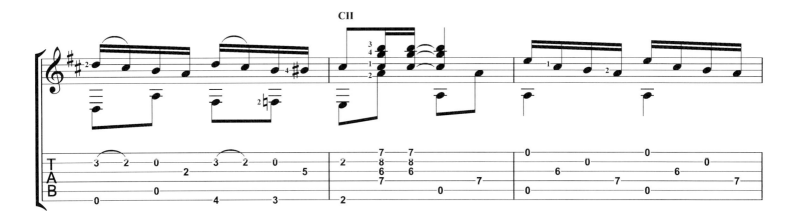

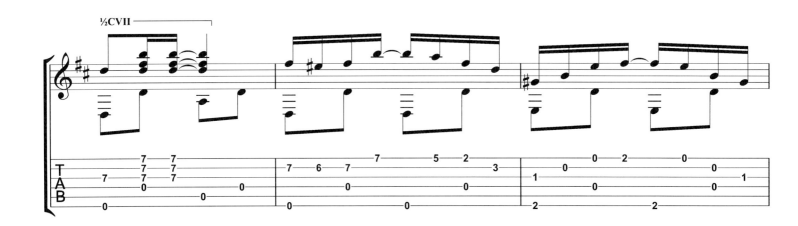

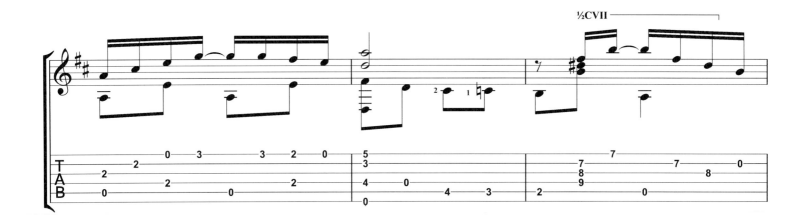

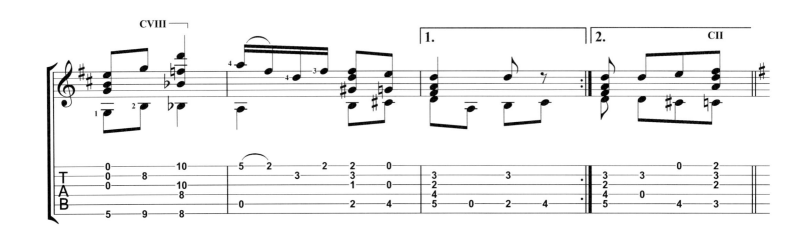

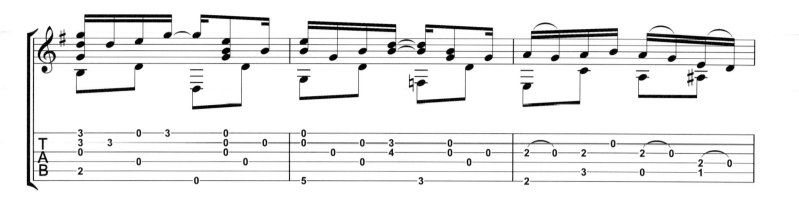

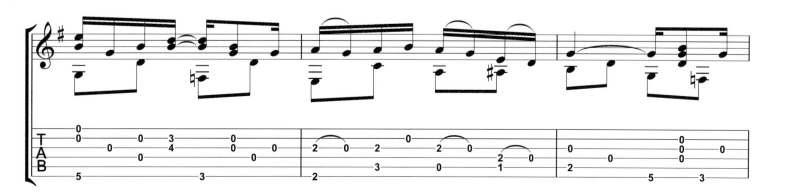

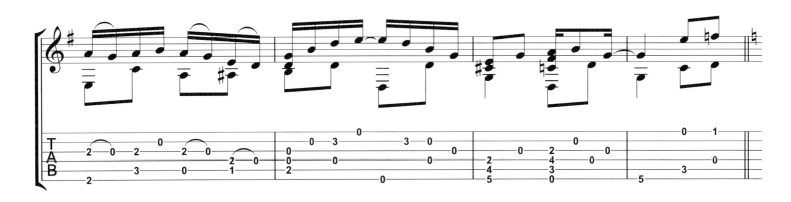

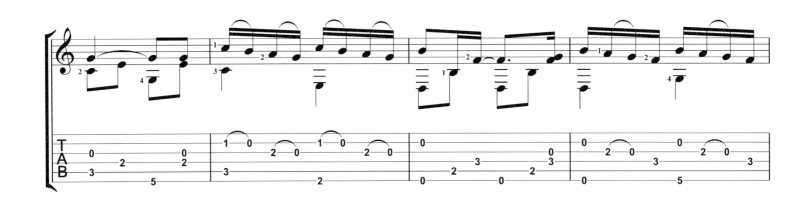

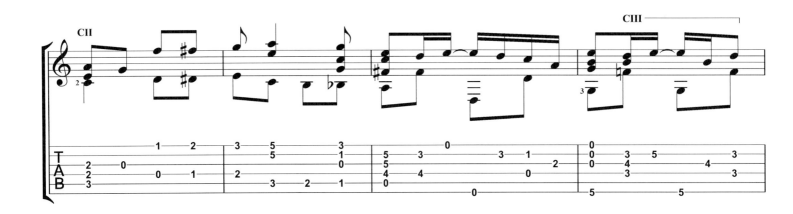

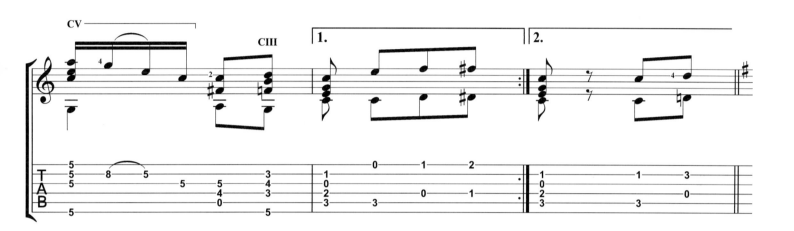

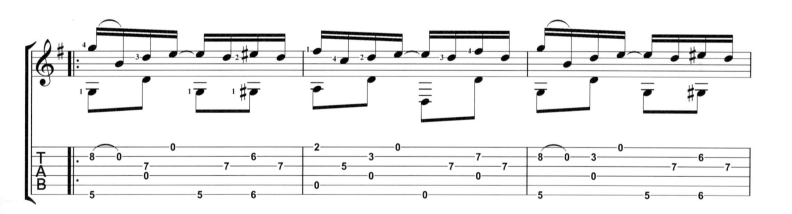

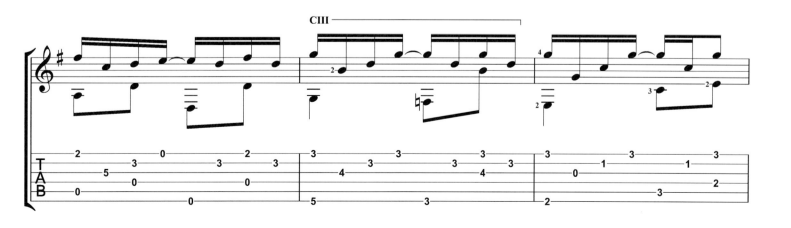

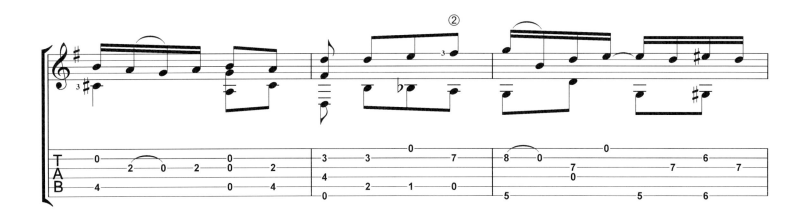

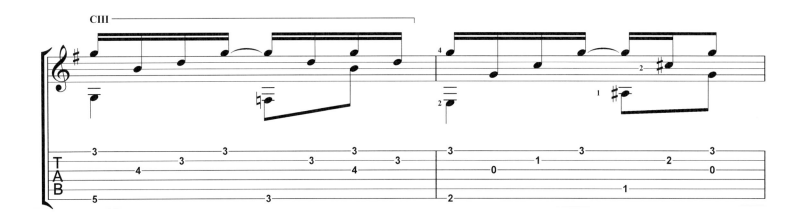

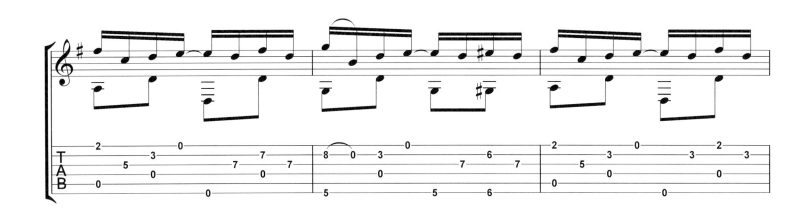

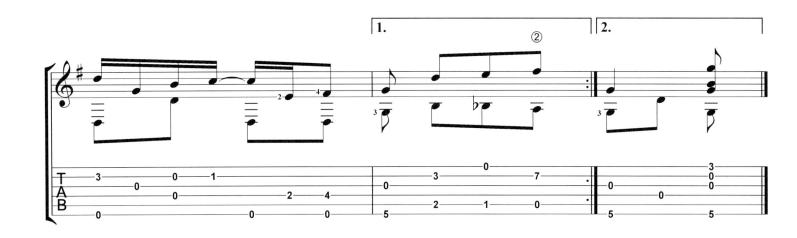

Maple Leaf Rag

Music by Scott Joplin

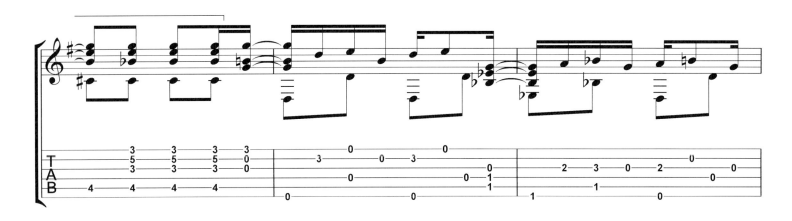

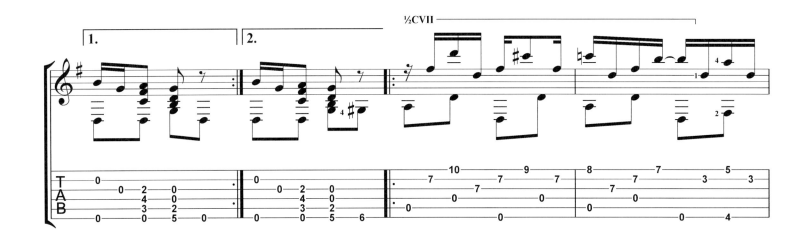

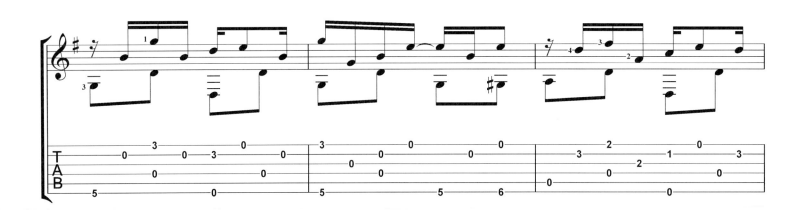

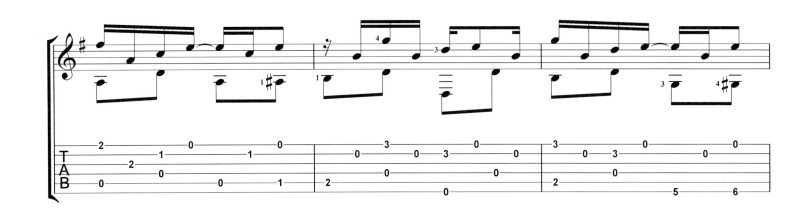

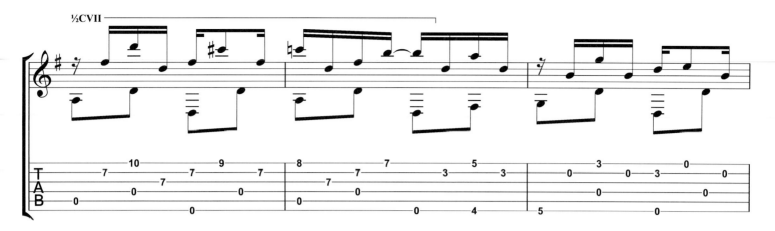

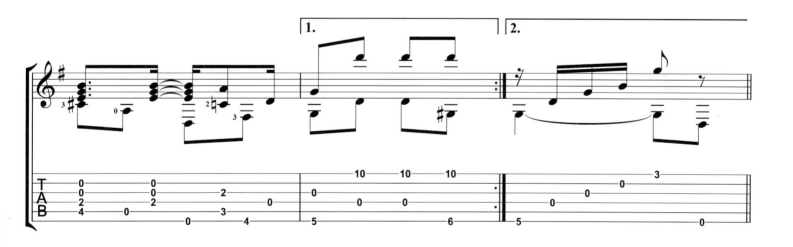

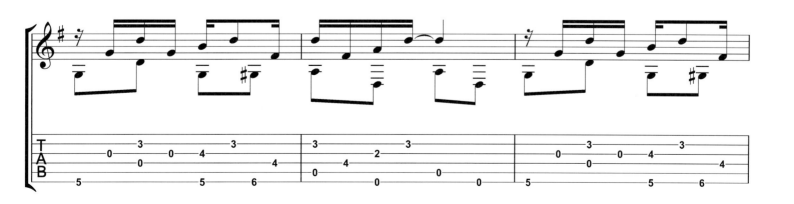

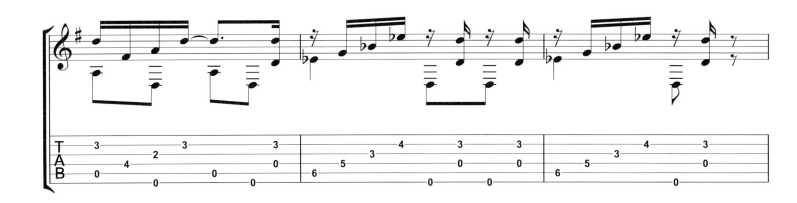

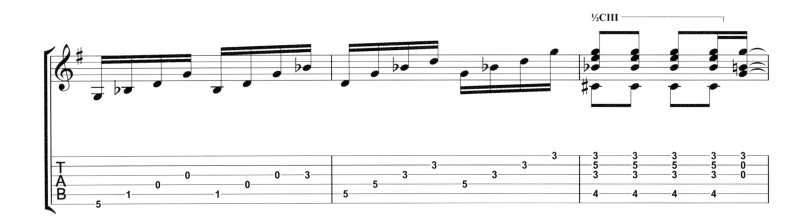

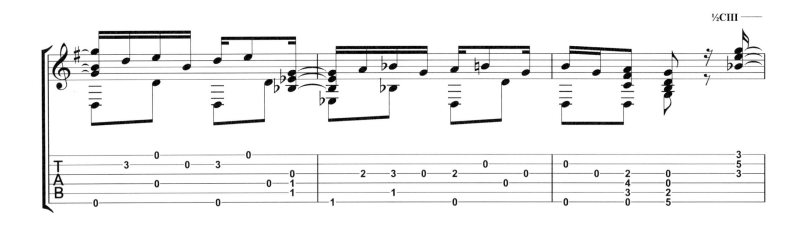

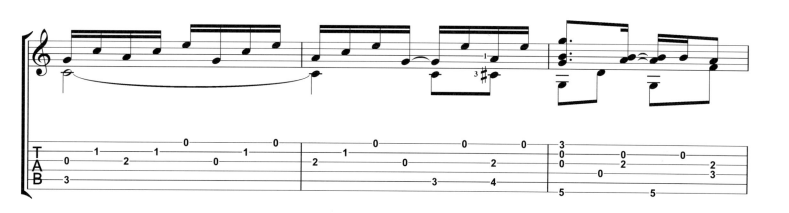

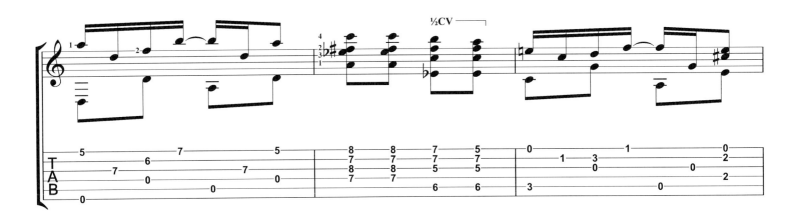

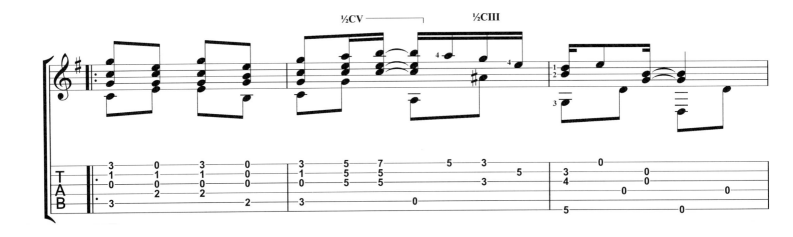

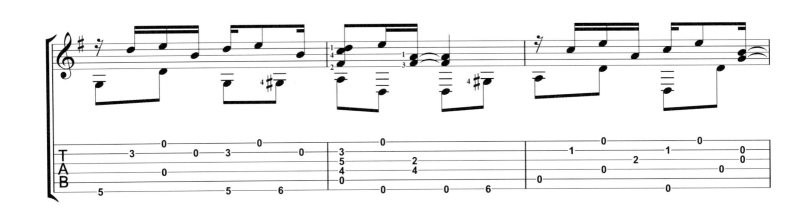

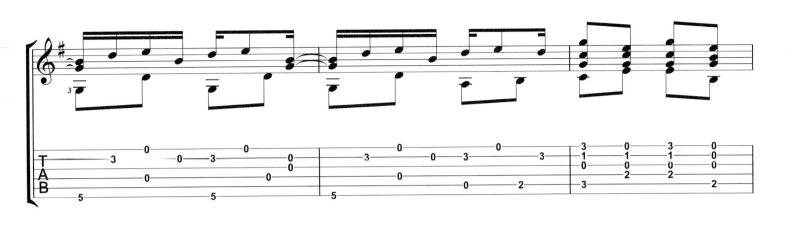

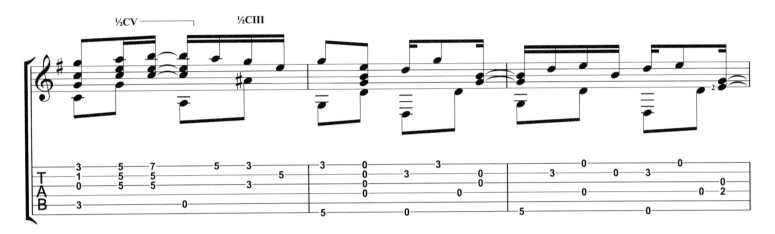

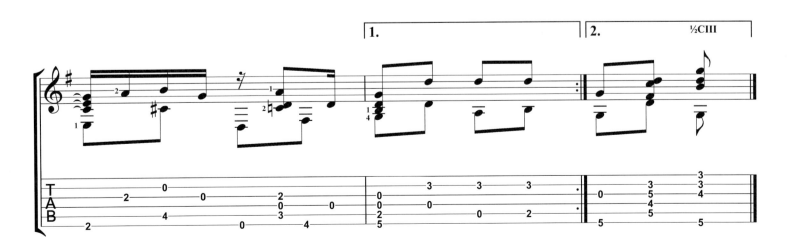

Pleasant Moments

Music by Scott Joplin

Capo 1

Slow waltz time

⑥ = D

The Strenuous Life

Music by Scott Joplin

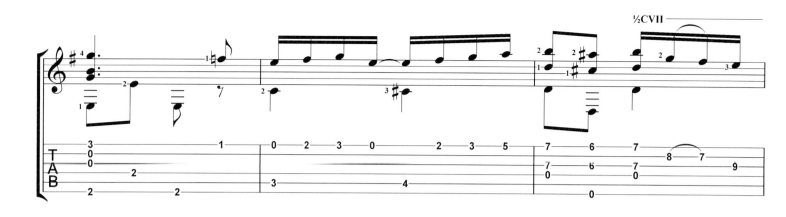

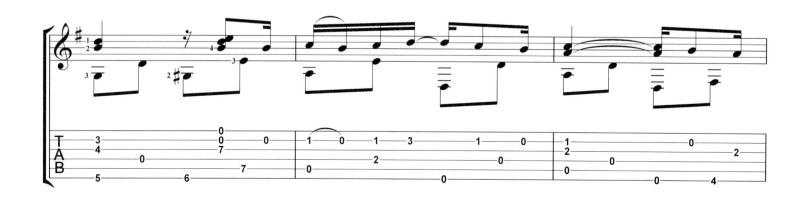

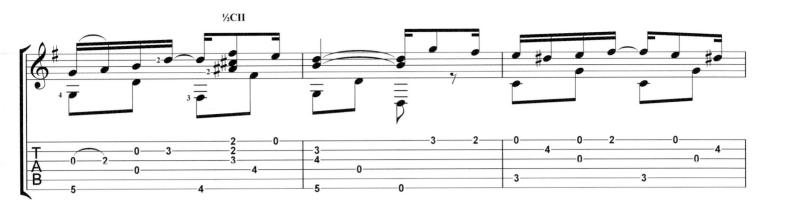

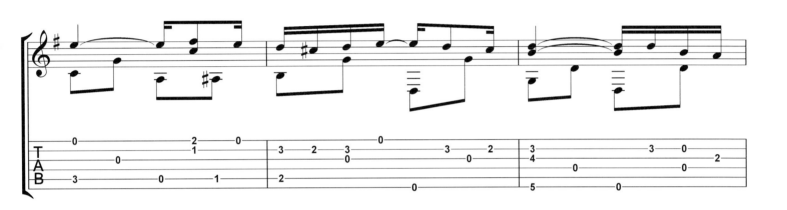

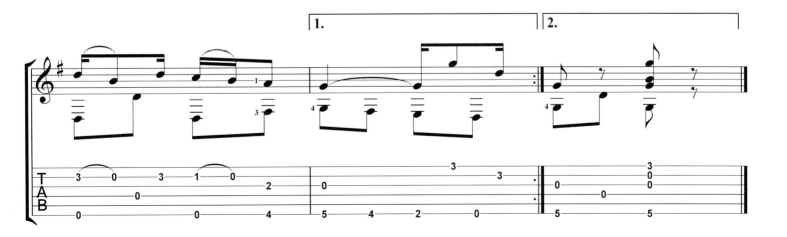

Something Doing

Music by Scott Joplin & Scott Hayden

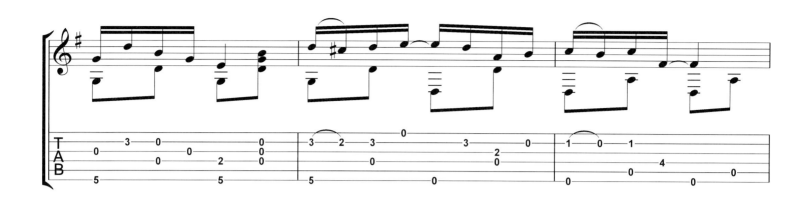

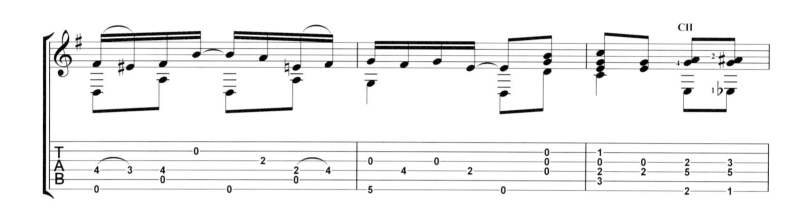

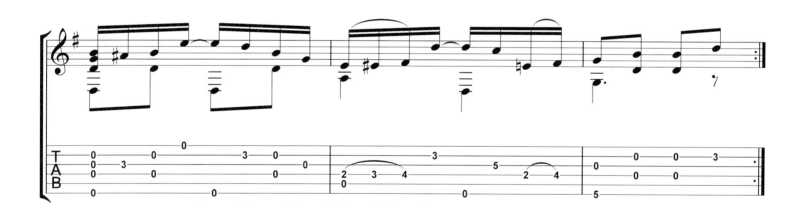

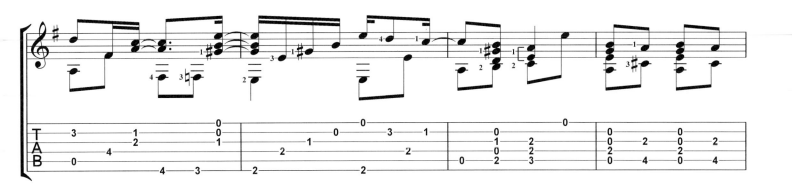

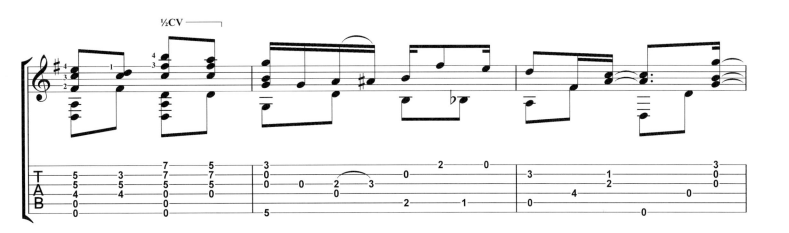

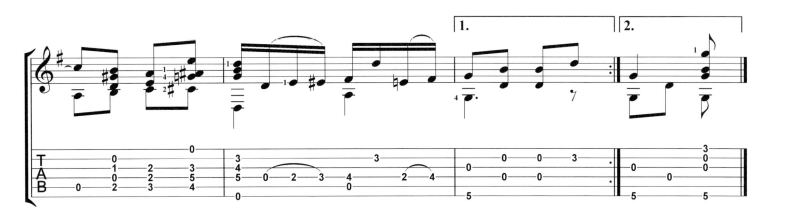

Sunflower Slow Drag

Music by Scott Joplin & Scott Hayden

56

Weeping Willow Rag

Music by Scott Joplin & Scott Hayden

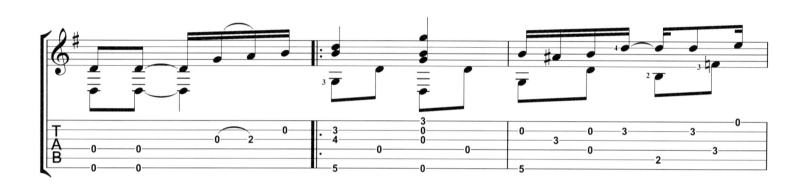

Edited by David Bradley.
Audio recorded by Jerry Willard.
Project editor: Adrian Hopkins.

Audio mixed and mastered by Jonas Persson.

Order No. AM1008315
ISBN: 978-1-78305-440-4

Exclusive Distributors:
Hal Leonard
7777 West Bluemound Road,
Milwaukee, WI 53213
Email: info@halleonard.com

Hal Leonard Europe Limited
42 Wigmore Street, Marylebone,
London WIU 2 RY
Email: info@halleonardeurope.com

Hal Leonard Australia Pty. Ltd.
4 Lentara Court, Cheltenham,
Victoria 9132, Australia
Email: info@halleonard.com.au

Printed in the EU.
www.halleonard.com